CENTRAL

D0397544

Learning
to Live
in the
World

Harcourt Brace & Company

SAN DIEGO NEW YORK LONDON

Learning to Live in the World

Earth Poems by William Stafford

CONTRA COSTA COUNTY LIBRARY

Selected by Jerry Watson and
Laura Apol Obbink

3 1901 03115 4695

Compilation and Introduction copyright © 1994 by Jerry Watson and Laura Apol Obbink

All rights reserved. No part of this publication may be reproduced or transmitted in any form or by any means, electronic or mechanical, including photocopy, recording, or any information storage and retrieval system, without permission in writing from the publisher.

Requests for permission to make copies of any part of the work should be mailed to: Permissions Department, Harcourt Brace & Company, 6277 Sea Harbor Drive, Orlando, Florida 32887-6777.

"Assurance," "Canadian," "Storm at the Coast," "Where We Live," "It's Like Wyoming," "West of Here," "The Coyote in the Zoo," and "Meditation" are copyright © 1978 by William Stafford. Reprinted from *Smoke's Way* with the permission of Graywolf Press, Saint Paul, MN. "Simple Talk," "Four Oak Leaves," "Starting with Little Things," "What If We Were Alone?," "Over the North Jetty," "Getting Scared," "The Bush from Mongolia," and "Why I Am Happy" are copyright © 1987 by William Stafford. Reprinted from *An Oregon Message* by permission of HarperCollins Publishers, Inc., New York, NY. "Listening Around," "The Day Millicent Found the World," "Climbing Along the River," "Life Work," "Some Things the World Gave," "The Dream of Now," "Five A.M.," "Yes," and "It's All Right" are copyright © 1991 by William Stafford. Reprinted from *Passwords* by permission of HarperCollins Publishers, Inc., New York, NY.

Library of Congress Cataloging-in-Publication Data
Stafford, William, 1914–1993.
Learning to live in the world: earth poems/by William Stafford;
selected by Jerry Watson and Laura Apol Obbink.
p. cm.
Summary: A collection of fifty poems that reflect the ways in which we relate to the world around us.
ISBN 0-15-200208-1
1. Children's poetry, American. [1. American poetry.]
I. Watson, Jerry. II. Obbink, Laura Apol. III. Title.
PS3537.T143A6 1994
811'.54—dc20 94-9900

The text was set in Galliard.
Title page photography by Kazuyuki Hashimoto/Photonica
Designed by David W. Blankenship
Printed in the United States of America
G F E D C B

Table of Contents

Introduction

William Stafford (1914–1993) was a poet exquisitely in tune with the world around him and deeply committed to exploring the place he occupied in that world. As a writer and teacher of writing, Stafford was above all a listener—a listener to the voices around and within him, a listener to the interplay of words and silences, and especially a listener to the earth itself. At the same time, he was blessed with the profound gift of putting what he heard and learned into words that we all can share.

Anyone who met Stafford recognized at once his openness and his gentle spirit. When talking about his writing, he often said that his attitude toward the ideas that came to him during his early morning writing time (usually beginning at 4:00 A.M.) was to greet those ideas at the door and to say, "Come in, come in!" And, indeed, that was very much the way Stafford treated his readers and his listeners—with a warm and welcoming smile, and with a willingness to take their questions, their conversations, and even their admiration quite seriously. Yet Stafford was not all gentleness; he could be fierce in his convictions and his commitments—not fierce in forcing them on others but fierce in articulating and adhering to them himself.

Stafford's writing can likewise be described as both gentle and fierce, both deceptively simple and highly complex. One of his stated ambitions was to help reduce the sense of distance people often feel between themselves and literature. And while his poems most certainly are literature, they are also poems that connect, poems that bridge the chasm between writer and reader, between the poet and the world.

This sense of connection runs throughout Stafford's life and his work—not only connection to readers but also connection to ideas and to the earth and its various inhabitants. Stafford was a prolific writer (he often said that he wrote at least a poem a day); *Learning to Live in the World* is only a sampling of his work. The pieces collected here were selected because they speak from a place and in a language that we believe can be recognized and understood by readers of many ages; the selections are unified by the themes of earth-loving and earth-keeping. We tried to include those poems that reflect Stafford's struggle with the world as well as his delight in, respect for, and engagement with the earth.

Because Stafford was a strong advocate of writing as a process of discovery, we allowed arranging this book to be for us a similar endeavor. As we began sorting through the volumes of his writing, we tried to let the poems speak to each other—to communicate, to congregate, and in the process to form patterns of their own. In the same way that Stafford said he trusted the writing process to guide him into clearer understandings of what he wanted to say, we trusted the coherence of Stafford's vision to guide us to an organization that made sense not only from the outside but from the inside as well.

As a result, the poems in *Learning to Live in the World* are grouped into five sections representing five different aspects of relating to the world; the section titles are taken from the poems themselves. The first section, "The World Speaks Everything to Us," conveys the idea of communication with and within the world. The second celebrates the connectedness of all of nature and is called "Even Far Things Are Real." "It Might Go Wild, Any Time" explains the wildness that is so much a part of the earth. "I See the Darkness; It Comes Near" articulates the pain and loss that is part of the human experience. And the fifth section, "You Live by the Light You Find," reveals the poet's sense of healing and hope.

William Stafford was committed to living in harmony with others and with the world; his voice and his vision are thus of increasing relevance to modern society. When this project originated, Stafford planned to write an afterword sharing his perspective on learning to live in the world. Although Stafford's death prevented him from writing that afterword, perhaps it was never really necessary, for the poet speaks eloquently and persuasively through his poems. His love for the earth, for its inhabitants, and for life itself resonates on every page.

—Laura Apol Obbink and Jerry Watson
February 1994

The World Speaks Everything to Us

EARTH DWELLER

It was all the clods at once become
precious; it was the barn, and the shed,
and the windmill, my hands, the crack
Arlie made in the axe handle: oh, let me stay
here humbly, forgotten, to rejoice in it all;
let the sun casually rise and set.
If I have not found the right place,
teach me; for, somewhere inside, the clods are
vaulted mansions, lines through the barn sing
for the saints forever, the shed and windmill
rear so glorious the sun shudders like a gong.

Now I know why people worship, carry around
magic emblems, wake up talking dreams
they teach to their children: the world speaks.
The world speaks everything to us.
It is our only friend.

THE DAY MILLICENT FOUND THE WORLD

Every morning Millicent ventured farther
into the woods. At first she stayed
near light, the edge where bushes grew, where
her way back appeared in glimpses among
dark trunks behind her. Then by farther paths
or openings where giant pines had fallen
she explored ever deeper into
the interior, till one day she stood under a great
dome among columns, the heart of the forest, and knew:
Lost. She had achieved a mysterious world
where any direction would yield only surprise.

And now not only the giant trees were strange
but the ground at her feet had a velvet nearness;
intricate lines on bark wove messages all
around her. Long strokes of golden sunlight
shifted over her feet and hands. She felt
caught up and breathing in a great powerful embrace.
A birdcall wandered forth at leisurely intervals
from an opening on her right: "Come away, Come away."
Never before had she let herself realize
that she was part of the world and that it would follow
wherever she went. She was part of its breath.

Aunt Dolbee called her back that time, a high
voice tapering faintly among the farthest trees,
"Milli-cent! Milli-cent!" And that time she returned,
but slowly, her dress fluttering along pressing
back branches, her feet stirring up the dark smell
of moss, and her face floating forward, a stranger's
face now, with a new depth in it, into the light.

Any Breeze to Willow:
   "You like to dance?"
Willow to Any Breeze:
   "Yes, oh yes."

Oak to Roots:
   "Think we can live?"
Roots to Oak:
   "Positive."

Dandelion Blossom:
   "When you're ready, say."
Dandelion Seed:
   "OK. OK."

Summer to Autumn:
   "Who carries my message to snow?"
Butterfly on a blossom:
   "When it's time, I'll go."

All to each other:
   "What to say to strong wind?"
Each other to All:
   "Be mine, Dear Friend."

NOTE

straw, feathers, dust—
little things

but if they all go one way,
that's the way the wind goes.

STARTING WITH LITTLE THINGS

Love the earth like a mole,
fur-near. Nearsighted,
hold close the clods,
their fine-print headlines.
Pat them with soft hands—

But spades, but pink and loving: they
break rock, nudge giants aside,
affable plow.
Fields are to touch:
each day nuzzle your way.

Tomorrow the world.

FOUR OAK LEAVES

1

When I was green, everyone loved me. Bees
crooned my sweetness; butterflies made me their own.
But then something called time began to drag me
away and I became curled up and brittle and brown.

2

These lines you read are what an oak leaf wrote,
following a storm that dragged it over the snow—
complaining and kicking. "I don't want to forsake
my tree. Help! Where did my sisters go?"

3

When spring comes, a whole new cast will have the stage
and I will huddle where winter threw me away,
but wherever I am the soil will be bitter because
I remember how lonely it was when I tried to stay.

4

This farewell comes from a forgiving leaf
that skipped with the others and then found a lucky storm
that brought me here. Listen—hold on as long
as you can, then trust forth: make truth your home.

SIMPLE TALK

Spilling themselves in the sun bluebirds
wing-mention their names all day. If everything
told so clear a life, maybe the sky would
come, maybe heaven; maybe appearance and
truth would be the same. Maybe whatever seems
to be so, we should speak so from our souls,
never afraid, "Light" when it comes,
"Dark" when it goes away.

WEEDS

What's down in the earth
comes forth in cold water,
in mist at night, in muttering
volcanoes that ring oceans
moving strangely at times.

And in autumn all the fields
witness forth: power there
where roots find it, rooms
delved silently and left
for the dark to have.

Up and down all highways
weed flags proclaim,
"Great is Earth our home!"
as we slip our hand
into winter's again.

Great is Earth our home.
Great is the sky.
And great are weeds in the fields.
We celebrate earth and air
as we sing in the wind.

ASK ME

Some time when the river is ice ask me
mistakes I have made. Ask me whether
what I have done is my life. Others
have come in their slow way into
my thought, and some have tried to help
or to hurt: ask me what difference
their strongest love or hate has made.

I will listen to what you say.
You and I can turn and look
at the silent river and wait. We know
the current is there, hidden; and there
are comings and goings from miles away
that hold the stillness exactly before us.
What the river says, that is what I say.

WHAT IF WE WERE ALONE?

What if there weren't any stars?
What if only the sun and the earth
circled alone in the sky? What if
no one ever found anything outside
this world right here?—no Galileo
could say, "Look—it is out there,
a hint of whether we are everything."

Look out at the stars. Yes—cold
space. Yes, we are so distant that
the mind goes hollow to think it.
But something is out there. Whatever
our limits, we are led outward. We glimpse
company. Each glittering point of light
beckons: "There is something beyond."

The moon rolls through the trees, rises
from them, and waits. In the river all
night a voice floats from rock
to sandbar, to log. What kind of listening
can follow quietly enough? We bow, and
the voice that falls through the rapids
calls all the rocks by their secret names.

Even Far Things Are Real

WHISPERED INTO THE GROUND

Where the wind ended and we came down
it was all grass. Some of us found
a way to the dirt—easy and rich.
When it rained, we grew, except
those of us caught up in leaves, not touching
earth, which always starts things.
Often we sent off our own
just as we'd done, floating that
wonderful wind that promised new land.

Here now spread low, flat on this
precious part of the world, we miss
those dreams and the strange old places
we left behind. We quietly wait.
The wind keeps telling us something
we want to pass on to the world:
Even far things are real.

Over these writings I bent my head.
Now you are considering them. If you
turn away I will look up: a bridge
that was there will be gone.
For the rest of your life I will stand here,
reaching across.

If these writings can bring a turn
or an echo that touches you—maybe
a face, a slant, a tune—you will stop
too and bend over them. When you
look up, your thought will reach
wherever I am.

I know it is strange. And there's no measure
for this. The only connection we make
is like a twinge when sometimes they change
the beat in music, and we sprawl with it
and hear another world for a minute
that is almost there.

WHERE WE LIVE

Inside a house I live, inside
a room that knowing makes, then
far inside something greater no one
can find or say.

And you live beside me,
millions of stars away.

CLIMBING ALONG THE RIVER

Willows never forget how it feels
to be young.

Do you remember where you came from?
Gravel remembers.

Even the upper end of the river
believes in the ocean.

Exactly at midnight
yesterday sighs away.

What I believe is,
all animals have one soul.

Over the land they love
they crisscross forever.

OUTSIDE

The least little sound sets the coyotes walking,
walking the edge of our comfortable earth.
We look inward, but all of them
are looking toward us as they walk the earth.

We need to let animals loose in our houses,
the wolf to escape with a pan in his teeth,
and streams of animals toward the horizon
racing with something silent in each mouth.

For all we have taken into our keeping
and polished with our hands belongs to a truth
greater than ours, in the animals' keeping.
Coyotes are circling around our truth.

The road goes down. It stops at the sea.
The sea goes on. It stops at the sky.
The sky goes on.

At the end of the road—picnickers,
rocks. We stand and look out:

Another sky where this one ends?
And another sea?
And a world, and a road?

And what about you?
And what about me?

CANADIAN

Hear the wild geese; know how their
eyes peer, feet fold into the down.
Open your eyes like that—see day
dawn at a certain height.

Hurt, cold, gleaming like
little stones high over the lakes,
the lakes in their heads pass, reading
the earth, finding the right wild place.

We can't be there; we can't
embrace what comes in a rush now,
now, while we hear the wild geese.

At sunset you have piled the empties and
come to the edge, where the wind kicks up
outside of town. A scatter of rain
rakes the desert. All this year's weather
whistles at once through the fence.

This land so wide, so gray, so still that
it carries you free—no one here need bother
except for their own breathing. You touch
a fencepost and the world steadies onward:
barbed wire, field, you, night.

GLIMPSE BETWEEN BUILDINGS

Now that the moon is out of a job
it has an easy climb, these nights,
finds an empty farm where a family could live,
slides wide over the forest—all those
million still violins before they are
carved—and follows those paths only air
ever uses. I feel my breath follow
those aisles and stumble on the moon
deep in forest pools. . . .

Moon, you old unsinkable submarine,
leaf admirer, be partly mine,
guide me tonight along city streets.
Help me do right.

STORM AT THE COAST

What moves on, moves far,
here. What holds, holds long.
But it is the wind and water will stay,
after the cliffs are gone.

WHY I AM HAPPY

Now has come, an easy time. I let it
roll. There is a lake somewhere
so blue and far nobody owns it.
A wind comes by and a willow listens
gracefully.

I hear all this, every summer. I laugh
and cry for every turn of the world,
its terribly cold, innocent spin.
That lake stays blue and free; it goes
on and on.

And I know where it is.

It Might Go Wild, Any Time

TORQUE

One day all the people come out on the street
and look at each other. Something is at
their throats, or as if a big magnet has hummed
and surrounded them with lines in the air.

Face gazes at face and then
up at the sky—nothing. Backs
arch, arms tighten and pull
out like limbs of trees, trembling.

But there is nothing. And it passes away.
People relax and stand there. The sun
is the same. Down the street a car
revs as usual. Nothing. Nothing.

Suppose this happens. The world looks
tame, but it might go wild, any time.

SITTING UP LATE

Beyond silence, on the other side merging
deep in the night, a wolf call lifted slowly
teasing farther than air extended,
thrilling into one pinpoint
across the ice.

The rest of my life
there never comes a simple feeling,
or warmth, or success, for always mingled
in the world is what I knew then
crystalized into a dark faith,
absolute,
between one breath and the next.

Even now in my hands the feel of the shovel comes back,
the shock of gravel or sand. Sun-scorch on my shoulders
bears down. The boss is walking around barking.
All the cement mixers rattle and jolt.

That day the trench we are digging goes deeper
and deeper, over my head; then the earth heaves
in one giant coffin gulp. They keep
digging and pulling and haul me out still breathing.

The sky, right there, was a precious cobalt dome
so near it pressed on my face. Beside me my hands
lay twitching and begging at the end of my arms.
Nothing is far anymore, after that trench, the stones. . . .

Oh near, and blessing again and again: my breath.
And the sky, and steady against my back, the earth.

OVER THE NORTH JETTY

Geese and brant, their wingbeat
steady—it's a long flight, Alaska—
bank their approach and then curve
upwind for landing. They live where storms
are so usual they are almost fair weather.

And we lean in that permanent gale,
watching those cold flocks depend on their wings
as they veer out of the north. In the last flight
one laggard pulls farther downwind
and peels off to disappear alone in the storm.

If you follow an individual away like that
a part of your life is lost forever,
beating somewhere in darkness, and belonging
only to storms that haunt around the world
on that risky path just over the wave.

LATER

Sometimes, loping along, I almost find
that band of sorrow the wolves found. Long nights
they steal forth where moonlight follows their breath;
they bring their faces near and let the whining
begin: it strings puppy and wolf together.
That long pang across the horizon tells
how a hunter called Man will come. In the night by a fire
their guttural plan will blaze. A banner of woe,
the wolf cry goes in the wind, lifting their moan.

Now they are almost extinguished. Their tendered song
has melted into The North, where trees and stones
wait for our song, when we meet in the cold
with our faces near and begin our low whine
that means we are on the trail the wolves have gone.

THE COYOTE IN THE ZOO

A yellow eye meets mine;
I suddenly know, too late,
the land outside belongs
to the one that looks away.

STORIES FROM KANSAS

Little bunches of
grass pretend they are bushes
that never will bow.
    They bow.

Carelessly the earth
escapes, loping out from the
timid little towns
    toward Colorado.

Which of the horses
we passed yesterday whinnied
all night in my dreams?
    I want that one.

THE BUSH FROM MONGOLIA

This bush with light green leaves
came from Mongolia where
it learned everything about wind.

All day and all night that cold lesson
clawed its firm hands everywhere
over whatever dared live above the ground.

These branches will never reach out
and celebrate the sun; these roots
will not relax their hold on the rocks.

Some of us have to be ready—
the big winter can come back, and only
bushes from Mongolia will survive.

THINGS THAT COME

After it came down from the mountains
the first house the wind found was ours—
tapped and rattled and pushed by curious
little pieces of air, and then shoved and
shaken by the wild-riding storm.

My father looked up—understood: that
voice in the night was tamed. Whatever struck
our house—let it come. He read on,
a story of a wolf and a man, a blizzard
where they warmed each other like friends.

There were other stories he promised he would
tell sometime; and we knew how far
he thought—his old home was blasted
away, and a bigger storm might come. He saved
us, though, that night, by how he cocked his head.

You think my poems are soft? That there isn't
a wolf in them? Listen—through all that swoop
down from the mountains my curious, quiet
breath comes: I am frantic to find these
little stones; I am building a house for us.

I See the Darkness; It Comes Near

REMEMBERING BROTHER BOB

Tell me, you years I had for my life,
tell me a day, that day it snowed
and I played hockey in the cold.
Bob was seven, then, and I was twelve,
and strong. The sun went down. I turned
and Bob was crying on the shore.

Do I remember kindness? Did I
shield my brother, comfort him?
Tell me, you years I had for my life.

Yes, I carried him. I took
him home. But I complained. I see
the darkness; it comes near: and Bob,
who is gone now, and the other kids.
I am the zero in the scene:
"You said you would be brave," I chided
him. "I'll not take you again."
Years, I look at the white across
this page, and think: I never did.

FALL WIND

Pods of summer crowd around the door;
I take them in the autumn of my hands.

Last night I heard the first cold wind outside;
the wind blew soft, and yet I shiver twice:

Once for thin walls, once for the sound of time.

TRAVELING THROUGH THE DARK

Traveling through the dark I found a deer
dead on the edge of the Wilson River road.
It is usually best to roll them into the canyon:
that road is narrow; to swerve might make more dead.

By glow of the tail-light I stumbled back of the car
and stood by the heap, a doe, a recent killing;
she had stiffened already, almost cold.
I dragged her off; she was large in the belly.

My fingers touching her side brought me the reason—
her side was warm; her fawn lay there waiting,
alive, still, never to be born.
Beside that mountain road I hesitated.

The car aimed ahead its lowered parking lights;
under the hood purred the steady engine.
I stood in the glare of the warm exhaust turning red;
around our group I could hear the wilderness listen.

I thought hard for us all—my only swerving—,
then pushed her over the edge into the river.

MEDITATION

Animals full of light
walk through the forest
toward someone aiming a gun
loaded with darkness.

That's the world: God
holding still
letting it happen again,
and again and again.

GETTING SCARED

Tending our fire in the oil drum, we felt
that second earthquake begin. Near dawn it was,
when everything stills. To be safe, we had
slept in a field. We felt a long slow wave
in the earth. It wasn't the stars that moved, but ourselves,
in time to a dance the dead could feel. Our fire
stirred where it cooled. Sparks whirled up.
Crawling along by a breath at a time, we tried to
get low; we tried to sight across level earth
near dawn and let the time tell us about how
to be alive in the grass, the miles, the strangeness,
with only the sun looking back from the other end of light.
We moved out as far as we could. "Forever," we thought,
"if we breathe too hard it will all be gone."
We spread our arms out wide on the ground
and held still. We set out for that cave we knew
above a stream, where early sunlight reaches
far back, willows all around, and clams in the river
for the taking. And we prayed for that steady event
we had loved so long without knowing it, our greatest
possession—the world when it didn't move.

OLD DOG

Toward the last in the morning she could not
get up, even when I rattled her pan.
I helped her into the yard, but she stumbled
and fell. I knew it was time.

The last night a mist drifted over the fields.
In the morning she would not raise her head—
the far, clear mountains we had walked
surged back to mind.

We looked a slow bargain: our days together
were the ones we had already had.
I gave her something the vet had given,
and patted her still, a good last friend.

BROKEN HOME

Here is a cup left empty in their
kitchen, a brim of that silent air,
all the cold mornings, all the cold years.

Here's an old jacket that held a scared heart
too loud for this house, hurt
in its pocket, wanting out.

How alone is this house!—an unreeled
phone dangling down a hall
that never really could lead to tomorrow.

CHILD IN THE EVENING

Why does this house have no windows, Mother?
Windows weaken a wall, My Son.

Why is it low, with nothing around?
The world is too bright and distracting, My Son.

Where are the neighbors, the friends, all gone?
They followed the years. They do that, My Son.

But I have sworn never to forsake them—
this place is lonely. I belong with my friends.
It is all right. They may come in.
This house is for everyone.

LATE AT NIGHT

Falling separate into the dark
the hailstone yelps of geese pattered
through our roof; startled we listened.

Those V's of direction swept by unseen
so orderly that we paused. But then
faltering back through their circle they came.

Were they lost up there in the night?
They always knew the way, we thought.
You looked at me across the room:—

We live in a terrible season.

You Live by the Light You Find

THE DREAM OF NOW

When you wake to the dream of now
from night and its other dream,
you carry day out of the dark
like a flame.

When spring comes north, and flowers
unfold from earth and its even sleep,
you lift summer on with your breath
lest it be lost ever so deep.

Your life you live by the light you find
and follow it on as well as you can,
carrying through darkness wherever you go
your one little fire that will start again.

SOME THINGS THE WORLD GAVE

1

Times in the morning early
when it rained and the long gray
buildings came forward from darkness
offering their windows for light.

2

Evenings out there on the plains
when sunset donated farms
that yearned so far to the west that the world
centered there and bowed down.

3

A teacher at a country school
walking home past a great marsh
where ducks came gliding in—
she saw the boy out hunting and waved.

4

Silence on a hill where the path ended
and then the forest below
moving in one long whisper
as evening touched the leaves.

5

Shelter in winter that day—
a storm coming, but in the lee
of an island in a cover with friends—
oh, little bright cup of sun.

IT'S ALL RIGHT

Someone you trusted has treated you bad.
Someone has used you to vent their ill temper.
Did you expect anything different?
Your work—better than some others'—has languished,
neglected. Or a job you tried was too hard,
and you failed. Maybe weather or bad luck
spoiled what you did. That grudge, held against you
for years after you patched up, has flared,
and you've lost a friend for a time. Things
at home aren't so good; on the job your spirits
have sunk. But just when the worst bears down
you find a pretty bubble in your soup at noon,
and outside at work a bird says, "Hi!"
Slowly the sun creeps along the floor;
it is coming your way. It touches your shoe.

Star Guides:
    Any star is enough
    if you know what star it is.

Kids:
    They dance before they learn
    there is anything that isn't music.

The Limbs of the Pin Oak Tree:
    "Gravity—what's that?"

An Argument Against the Empirical Method:
    Some haystacks don't even have any needle.

Comfort:
    We think it is calm here,
    or that our storm is the right size.

FIVE A.M.

Still dark, the early morning breathes
a soft sound above the fire. Hooded
lights on porches lead past lawns,
a hedge; I pass the house of the couple
who have the baby, the yard with the little
dog; my feet pad and grit on the pavement, flicker
past streetlights; my arms alternate
easily to my pace. Where are my troubles?

There are people in every country who never
turn into killers, saints have built
sanctuaries on islands and in valleys,
conquerors have quit and gone home, for thousands
of years farmers have worked their fields.
My feet begin the uphill curve
where a thicket spills with birds every spring.
The air doesn't stir. Rain touches my face.

ONE TIME

When evening had flowed between houses
and paused on the schoolground, I met
Hilary's blind little sister following
the gray smooth railing still warm from the sun
with her hand; and she stood by the edge
holding her face upward waiting
while the last light found her cheek
and her hair, and then on over the trees.

You could hear the great sprinkler arm
of water find and then leave the pavement,
and pigeons telling each other their dreams
or the dreams they would have. We were
deep in the well of shadow by then, and I
held out my hand, saying, "Tina, it's me—
Hilary says I should tell you it's dark,
and, oh, Tina, it is. Together now—"

And I reached, our hands touched,
and we found our way home.

FRIENDS

How far friends are! They forget you,
most days. They have to, I know; but still,
it's lonely just being far and a friend.
I put my hand out—this chair, this table—
so near: touch, that's how to live.
Call up a friend? All right, but the phone
itself is what loves you, warm on your ear,
on your hand. Or, you lift a pen
to write—it's not that far person
but this familiar pen that comforts.
Near things: Friend, here's my hand.

Consider the slow descent
that a dandelion puff once found
(a plane had carried it so far away
you couldn't imagine it could come down)—

Afloat in space hardly even air
that wavery journey began—
a slight parachute, no center at all,
a nothing that follows the slightest wind.

"Now where might Earth turn gold?" it says,
"that the Midas touch may not be gone."
(One seed could make a meadow glow:
the slow decisioning descends.)

It comes down mixed with snow, a seed
from far that hitched with wind,
and your sweater sleeve is for landing on
(and you are not doing important things).

That seedflake melts without a trace,
that golden touch, Midas for friend—
but it brushes your sleeve in the right place
and your life becomes important again.

YES

It could happen any time, tornado,
earthquake, Armageddon. It could happen.
Or sunshine, love, salvation.

It could, you know. That's why we wake
and look out—no guarantees
in this life.

But some bonuses, like morning,
like right now, like noon,
like evening.

ASSURANCE

You will never be alone, you hear so deep
a sound when autumn comes. Yellow
pulls across the hills and thrums,
or the silence after lightning before it says
its names—and then the clouds' wide-mouthed
apologies. You were aimed from birth:
you will never be alone. Rain
will come, a gutter filled, an Amazon,
long aisles—you never heard so deep a sound,
moss on rock, and years. You turn your head—
that's what the silence meant: *you're not alone.*
The whole wide world pours down.

Epilogue

REMINDERS

Before dawn, across the whole road
as I pass I feel spiderwebs.

Within people's voices, under their words or
woven into the pauses, I hear a hidden sound.

One thin green light flashes over a smooth sea
just as the sun goes down.

What roses lie on the altar of evening
I inhale carefully, to keep more of.

Tasting all these and letting them have
their ways to waken me, I shiver and resolve:

In my life, I will more than live.

Index of Titles

Index of First Lines